BRANCH LINES AROUND EFFINGHAM JUNCTION

including the Hampton Court branch

Vic Mitchell and Keith Smith

MP Middleton Press

Cover picture: Class M7 0-4-4T no.22 runs into Effingham Junction on 4th April 1925, while the new conductor rail insulators are still clean. A horse box is between the locomotive and the four-coach set. (H.C.Casserley)

First published April 1990

ISBN 0 906520 74 6

© Middleton Press 1990

Design and Laser typesetting - Deborah Goodridge

Published by Middleton Press
          Easebourne Lane
          Midhurst, West Sussex
          GU29 9AZ
          Tel. (0730) 813169

Printed & bound by Biddles Ltd,
          Guildford and Kings Lynn

CONTENTS

GEOGRAPHICAL SETTING

The Hampton Court branch climbs gently away from the River Thames to reach the main line at Hampton Court Junction. From there the Effingham Junction line takes an undulating path and crosses the River Mole, south of Cobham. This river also passes under the railway at Leatherhead and at Hampton Court, where it joins the Thames. Most of the lines were built on London Clay, which had some economic value for brickmaking. At Guildford, the geography presented the railway builders with more work than elsewhere, as they had to construct substantial embankments and a short viaduct in order to traverse the Wey Valley.

ACKNOWLEDGEMENTS

We are extremely grateful for the assistance received from many of the photographers mentioned in the captions and also from R.M.Casserley, Dr.E.Course, G.Croughton, J.Janaway, N.Langridge, Mrs.M.Mason, T.Patrick, R.Randell, G.T.V.Stacey, E.Staff, N.Stanyon, D.Wallis, L.Whisstock and our ever helpful wives.

SOUTHERN RAILWAY.
TOTALISATOR STAFF.
(2) London to (2)
HAMPTON COURT
by Rail (Third Class), thence by
Messrs Classique Coaches Ltd.
to Hurst Park Race Course
AND £RETURN.
18th. MAY 1937
FOR CONDITIONS SEE BACK.
0100

All the maps are to the scale of 25" to 1 mile, unless otherwise stated.

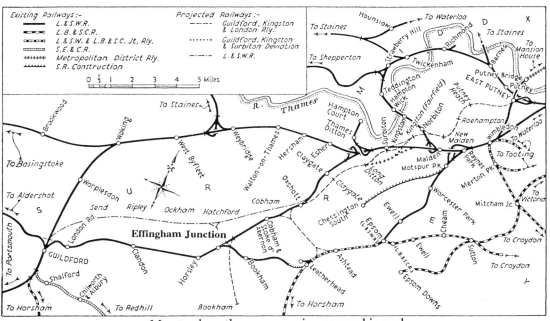

Map to show the pre-grouping ownership and some of the proposed railways in the area.
(Railway Magazine)

HISTORICAL BACKGROUND

The first line in the area was that between London (Nine Elms) and Woking (Common), and it opened on the 21st May 1838. The branch to Hampton Court followed on 1st February 1849. These routes were operated by the London & South Western Railway, which completed another branch from its main line in 1859, south to Leatherhead. This line was operated jointly with the London, Brighton & South Coast Railway between Epsom and Leatherhead. The branch from Woking to Guildford came into use on 5th May 1845.

In the ensuing years, a large number of schemes were drawn up for railways to be built in the area between these lines, but it was not until 2nd February 1885 that the routes between Leatherhead, Guildford and Hampton Court Junction came into use. The term "Guildford New Line" was applied between the latter two places and is still used today.

Electrification of LSWR suburban services started in 1915, reaching Hampton Court on 18th June 1916 and Claygate on 20th November 1916. World War I prevented extensions of the scheme and its after effects caused withdrawal of the Claygate electric trains in June 1919. On 12th July 1925, electric services commenced on the routes from Waterloo to Guildford (via Cobham) and to Effingham Junction (via Leatherhead).

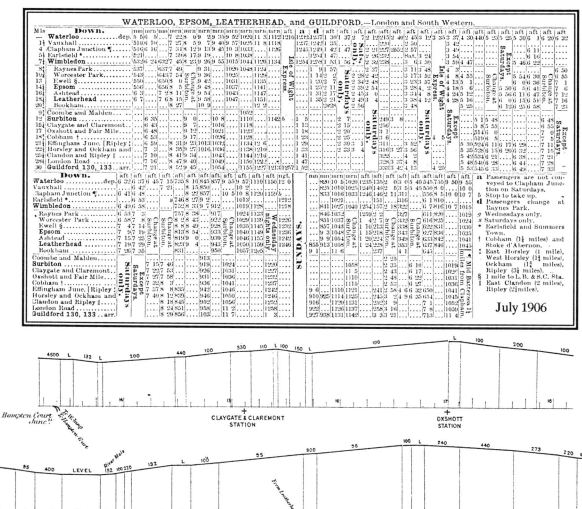

WATERLOO, EPSOM, LEATHERHEAD, and GUILDFORD.—London and South Western.

July 1906

PASSENGER SERVICES

The first timetable gave twelve weekday and four Sunday trains between Waterloo and Guildford on the new routes, half running via Cobham and half via Bookham. By 1906, 14 trains called at Bookham and 13 at Cobham on weekdays, although some of the former terminated at Horsley. There were five and four journeys on each route on Sundays, respectively. From 1890, a number of Portsmouth trains travelled via Cobham, there being five down and three up by 1913.

The 1917 timetable showed a basic 30 minute interval electric service between Waterloo and Claygate, connecting with an hourly steam push-pull service to Guildford on weekdays. On Sundays, this operated through to Surbiton. The Bookham route was served by an hourly Waterloo-Horsley service, which was two-hourly on Sundays. There were a few peak hour through trains.

After the withdrawal of electric services to Claygate in mid-1919 until the introduction of the all electric timetable in July 1925, there were steam trains hourly, every day, between Waterloo and Guildford (via Cobham) and Waterloo and Horsley (via Bookham).

Initially, electric trains ran at 20 minute intervals (30 minutes on Sundays) between Waterloo and Guildford, via Cobham. An hourly service was provided daily, between Waterloo and Effingham Junction via Bookham, with a similar one from London Bridge via Mitcham Junction, supplemented on Summer Sundays by through trains from Victoria to Guildford. Apart from curtailments during and after World War II, a similar frequency was maintained until September 1958, when the interval was increased from 20 to 30 minutes. In recent years all Central Division services via Bookham (latterly from Victoria) have been discontinued and the off-peak frequency reduced to an hourly train from Waterloo.

Further examples of regular working of Portsmouth trains have occurred. Between 1956 and 1959 the 7.33 am from Portsmouth Harbour ran between Guildford and Waterloo via Cobham, stopping only at Surbiton. The 09.52 up stopping service from Guildford via Cobham originated at Portsmouth from 1978 until 1986, as did the 16.52 in 1978-89. Similarly, departures from Waterloo via Cobham were extended to Portsmouth at 08.30 (1978-87), 15.30 (1979-86) and 16.30 (1978-86). These through trains operated Monday to Friday only.

The timetable from May 1990 shows the most dramatic change in the history of the lines - a new service from Guildford to North London and Luton via Effingham Junction, Leatherhead, Sutton and the Thameslink route.

Hampton Court Branch

An infrequent service was provided initially. By 1869, there were 15 weekday and 11 Sunday trains to and from Waterloo, only one down train failing to stop at Thames Ditton. In 1890, the branch was handling 24 trains on weekdays and 12 on Sundays. The figures for July 1906 were 27 and 22, respectively. Until 1936 there was a semi-fast steam train from Hampton Court each morning, largely to bring stock up to Waterloo for a down Portsmouth service. Doubts that the M7 tanks would be able to surmount the new Wimbledon flyover then led to its replacement by an electric train.

From 1916 until 1958, a basic 15 or 20 minute interval service was operated, apart from reductions made due to the effects of war. Subsequently trains have called at all stations to Waterloo, every 30 minutes.

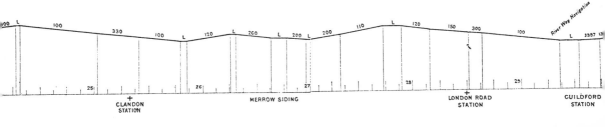

HAMPTON COURT

1. Hampton Court Palace was presented to King Henry VIII in 1526. Its architectural charm and outstanding gardens having since attracted hordes of visitors, the majority arriving by rail until the advent of the electric tramway in 1903. This awning was erected in 1899. (Lens of Sutton)

3. In 1949, the pre-grouping wooden bodied EMUs were to be seen running with a new and wider all steel coach incorporated to form a 4-car set. Beyond is a 2NOL, the furthest coach of which is against a short platform. Platform 1 (centre) had been shortened and the concourse widened, after the platform numbers had been reversed in August 1934. (J.H.Aston)

2. The main station buildings are seen to the right of the signal box, as class M7 0-4-4T no.23 clatters over the crossover. This 45-lever box was in use from 1899 until 1958. At its zenith, the station would receive up to 50 extra trains on Bank Holidays. (S.C.Nash coll.)

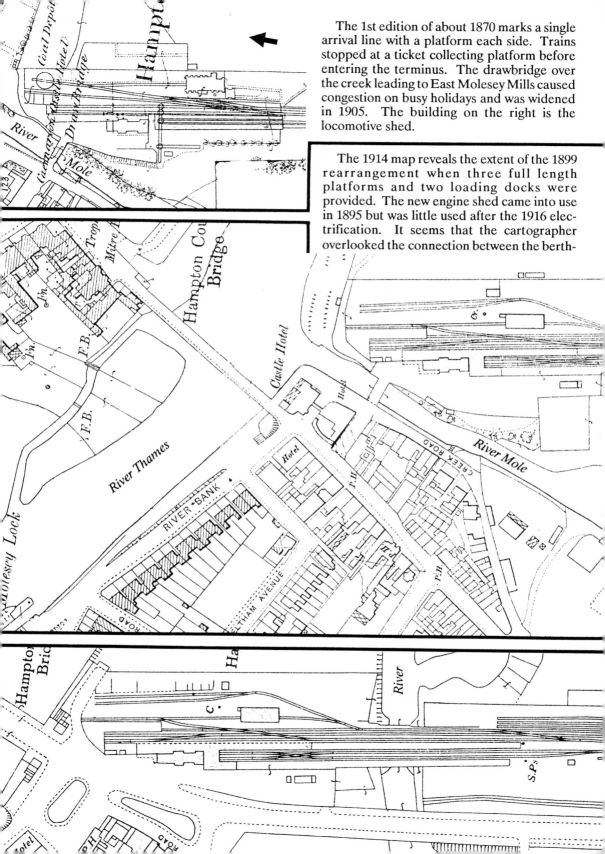

The 1st edition of about 1870 marks a single arrival line with a platform each side. Trains stopped at a ticket collecting platform before entering the terminus. The drawbridge over the creek leading to East Molesey Mills caused congestion on busy holidays and was widened in 1905. The building on the right is the locomotive shed.

The 1914 map reveals the extent of the 1899 rearrangement when three full length platforms and two loading docks were provided. The new engine shed came into use in 1895 but was little used after the 1916 electrification. It seems that the cartographer overlooked the connection between the berth-

The 1897 survey shows that the locomotive turntable had been removed and that the line was extended onto a riverfront wharf. The wagon turntables to the small goods yard and shed remained, wagons being moved manually or by horse. The drawings for the conversion of the locomotive shed into a goods shed were dated 16th July 1895.

ing sidings and the up line, near Hampton Court Crossing Box (right). Note the wider road bridge leading to the station, which was then still situated on an island. Molesey Lock is shown, this being the destination of passengers with circular tour tickets that included a steamer trip to Windsor.

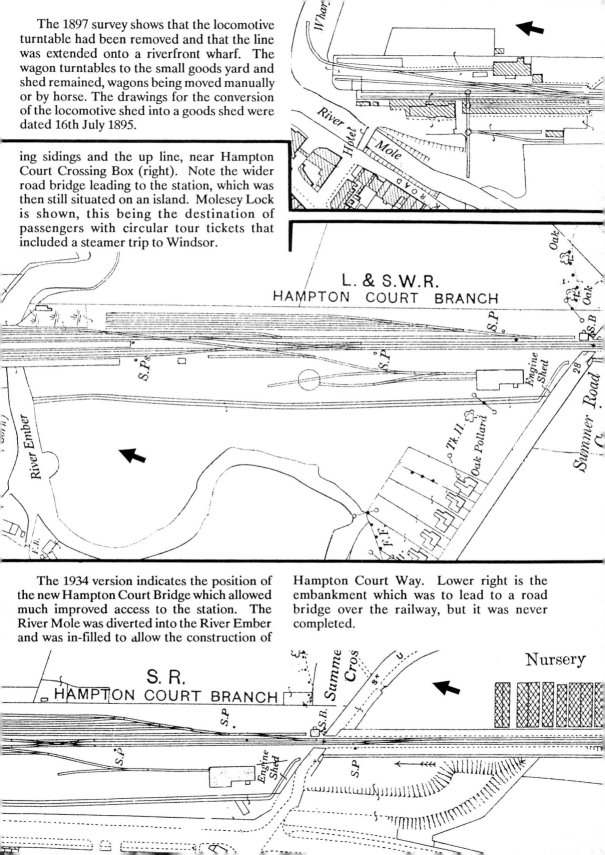

L. & S.W.R.
HAMPTON COURT BRANCH

The 1934 version indicates the position of the new Hampton Court Bridge which allowed much improved access to the station. The River Mole was diverted into the River Ember and was in-filled to allow the construction of Hampton Court Way. Lower right is the embankment which was to lead to a road bridge over the railway, but it was never completed.

S. R.
HAMPTON COURT BRANCH

Nursery

4. The twenty lever frame of Hampton Court Crossing Box was dramatically repositioned in October 1947, when an EMU over ran the shunting neck in fog. Hampton Court Palace is visible in the left background. (J.H.Aston)

5. This ramshackle affair was erected on the other side of the road - 1947 was a time of extreme austerity, when even wood was rationed. It remained in use until 1957. (J.N.Faulkner)

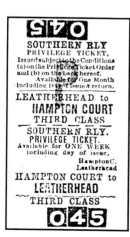

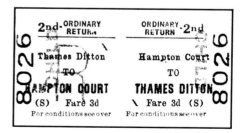

6. A new box by the crossing came into use on 3rd March 1957, taking over the functions of the station box on 14th September 1958. On 1st March 1970, it became a gate box only and from 29th July 1979 it controlled barriers, but these were operated under CCTV from Surbiton Panel from 23rd September 1979. The roof of the former engine shed is visible through the trees. (D.Cullum)

7. The down home signals are seen in 1954, prior to the provision of a route indicator displaying the platform numbers. The goods yard signal (right) was retained and a calling-on arm provided. (R.C.J.Day)

→

9. In the 1840s, the Office of Works required that the railway buildings should be in keeping with the Tudor palace on the opposite bank of the river. Although not added until the turn of the century, the little goods office was of the same style. The goods yard closed on 3rd May 1965, just after this photograph had been taken. (J.N.Faulkner)

8. There was a rare appearance of steam on 2nd December 1962, when Beattie 2-4-0WTs nos. 30585 and 30587 arrived with a RCTS/SLS railtour. Unfortunately they were short of water and with the station hoses frozen, the fire brigade had to be summoned. (T.Wright)

10. Of the four berthing sidings, three were electrified, as can be seen in this 1971 view. The two on the right were in use from 1908 until 1971 - none now exist. Back in 1937, the SR carried 62,000 passengers for Hurst Park Races in a single day! (R.E.Ruffell)

11. The canopy on platform 1 was cut back in the 1930s and that over nos. 2 and 3 in the 1960s. All platforms are boarded where they pass over the river. Prototype 4PEP no. 4001 stands with 4SUB no. 4719 on 24th September 1973. (J.Scrace)

12. Pictured in 1973, the main building was only partially used in 1990 - a ticket office at the north end and a newsagent in the middle. Serious cracking was then evident and most windows were boarded up. The station is situated in East Molesey, Hampton Court being north of the river. (J.Scrace)

British Rail Hampton Court

THAMES DITTON

13. Built on an embankment, the station was opened in November 1851 to serve the nearby riverside village. This view towards the junction shows the "signal box" window, the six levers being situated in the main building. The box closed on 24th April 1960.
(Lens of Sutton)

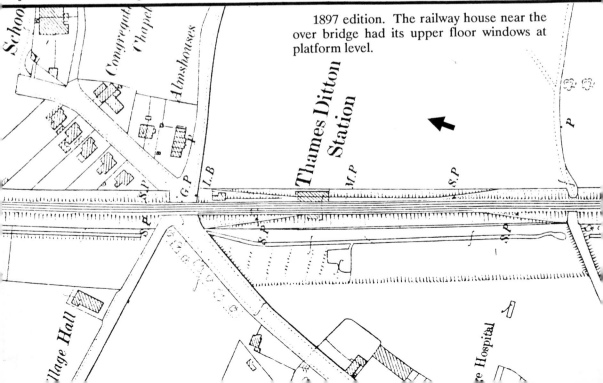

1897 edition. The railway house near the over bridge had its upper floor windows at platform level.

14. Another southward view features empty stock of 1925 build passing through on 10th June 1957. The up signals are "on" - a rare occurrence, as the signal box was manned only one day each year. This was Whit Monday when Hurst Park Races were held. (J.N.Faulkner)

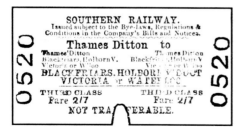

16. Hampton Court was a favourite venue for excursions, which often included a steamer cruise. Here we witness no. 33007 returning with a special to Bury, Lancs. (J.N.Faulkner)

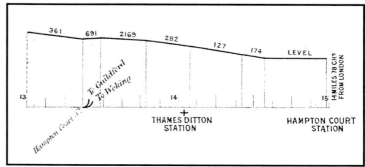

15. The branch freight returns to Surbiton on 12th April 1958, hauled by U class 4-6-0 no. 31624. The sign mentions Trianco, the well known manufacturer of domestic boilers. Another local firm of note was AC Cars, manufacturers of sports cars, invalid cars and railcars. (J.N.Faulkner)

HAMPTON COURT JUNCTION

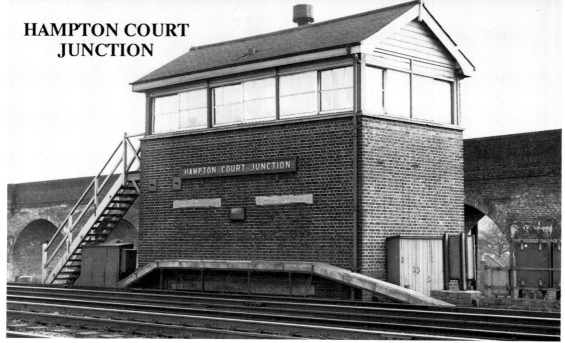

17. A flyunder for up Cobham line trains came into use on 21st October 1908 and a flyover for down Hampton Court services followed on 4th July 1915. The down Hampton Court line is behind the signal box in this 1970 photograph. The 1936 box closed on 1st March of that year, having nearly been destroyed by a V2 rocket in 1944. (J.Scrace)

Maps and other photographs of this junction can be seen in our *Waterloo to Woking* album.

18. On 23rd February 1979, a train from Hampton Court passed an adverse signal and struck a glancing blow to an up stopping train from Woking. In the foreground is the multi-gauge track of the Malden & District Society of Model Engineers, the structure obscuring their ground level track.
(D.Stamp coll.)

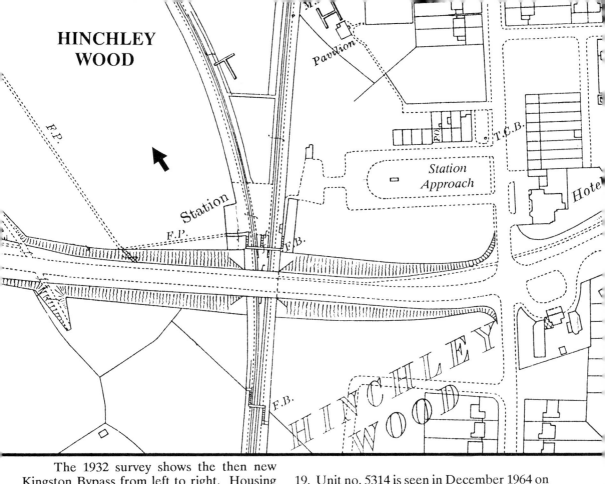

HINCHLEY WOOD

FP.

Pavilion

Station Approach

P.O.

T.C.B.

Station

Hotel

F.P.

F.B.

F.B.

HINCHLEY WOOD

The 1932 survey shows the then new Kingston Bypass from left to right. Housing development in the area was rapid and by the 1970s the area was so busy that a bypass was needed for the bypass.

19. Unit no. 5314 is seen in December 1964 on the single down track, north of the station. Adjacent is the trackbed of the up line, in use until 1908. (J.N.Faulkner)

20. The station was opened on 20th October 1930, access being by means of a footbridge, except for staff who could cross the down line in the foreground. (J.Scrace)

21. Another May 1989 photograph shows the curved up platform and the ticket office at the foot of the steps. The steps on the left now give access to a residential area. (J.Scrace)

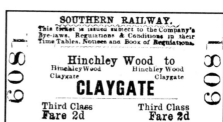

SOUTHERN RAILWAY.
This ticket is issued subject to the Company's Bye-laws, Regulations & Conditions in their Time Tables, Notices and Book of Regulations.

Hinchley Wood to
Hinchley Wood   Hinchley Wood
Claygate   Claygate
CLAYGATE

Third Class   Third Class
Fare 2d   Fare 2d

6081   1809

CLAYGATE

22. Opened with the line, the station did much to encourage the development of good quality housing in the district, the population now being about 7000. This postcard view towards London shows the goods yard in the background. (Lens of Sutton)

The 1932 survey includes the beginning of the up refuge siding (lower right), which was added in 1897 prior to the introduction of fast Portsmouth trains to the route. In 1990, there were still entrances to both sides of the station and a crossover at the London end.

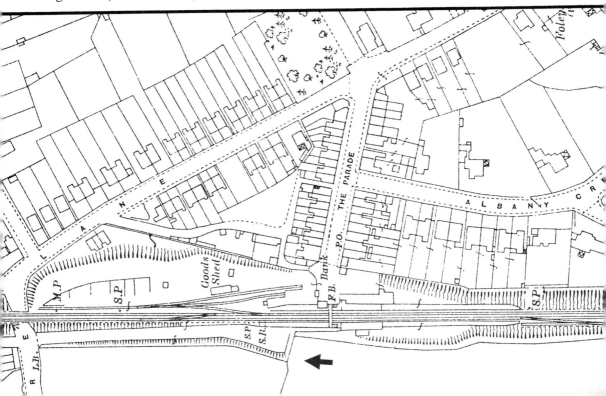

23. The upper quadrant signal peeps above the footbridge which was probably heavily used in 1916-19, when electric trains from London presumably terminated in the down platform and push-pull steam trains from Guildford did likewise on the up side. (Lens of Sutton)

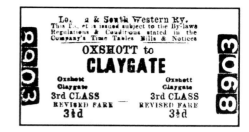

London & South Western Ry.
This Ticket is issued subject to the By-laws Regulations & Conditions stated in the Company's Time Tables Bills & Notices

OXSHOTT to
CLAYGATE

Oxshott Claygate	Oxshott Claygate
3rd CLASS	3rd CLASS
REVISED FARE	REVISED FARE
3½d	3½d

24. The 7.33am Portsmouth Harbour to Waterloo speeds through on 11th October 1958, composed of one 4RES and two 4COR units, the centre one including the restaurant car. It took only two minutes longer than the fast trains running via Woking. (J.N.Faulkner)

25. At this time, the box was only opened for the passing of the fast train, shown in the previous picture, and for the shunting of the goods yard, which closed on the 6th May 1963. The box was abolished on 22nd March 1969. (J.N.Faulkner)

OXSHOTT

26. Although one of the original stations, it did not receive a footbridge until 1900. With the Bagshot Beds of Oxshott Heath and Esher Common to the north, most of the passengers emanated from well spaced houses to the south of the station. (Lens of Sutton)

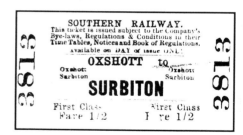

27. As late as May 1954, lower quadrant ex-LSWR signals were still serving as down starters. The white quadrants eliminated the risk of setting sun giving a green signal. (D.Cullum coll.)

28. No. S5124 leads the 4.12pm from Waterloo on 20th August 1955 and was typical of the stock in use on the route in that and the subsequent two decades. The signal box was in operation until 21st April 1963. (J.H.Aston)

29. Portsmouth expresses are frequently diverted onto the route, as witnessed on 1st October 1967. The up signal was missing at this time as Cooks Crossing Box had become a block post, prior to the introduction of colour light signals in 1970. (J.N.Faulkner)

30. Photographed in 1989, the station retained its dignity and was freshly painted. For many years a Metropolitan coal dues obelisk was visible at the top of the cutting in the distance. A coal tax was payable until 1890, having been levied for about 600 years. (J.Scrace)

The 1934 map marks a pair of railway cottages between the station and Oxshott Heath, which is north of the station.

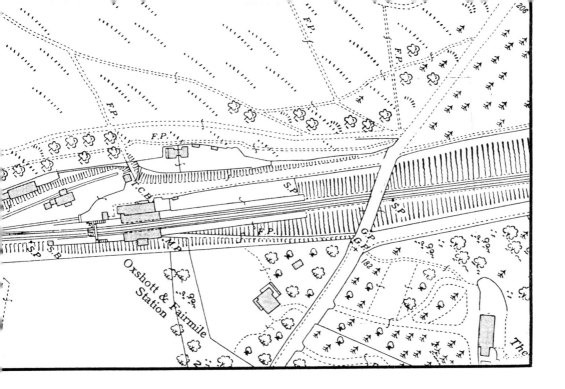

31. The north elevation in 1989 also gave the appearance of a well cared for station and station house. The former goods yard now forms a car park which has an extension at a higher level. (J.Scrace)

SOUTH OF OXSHOTT

32. Sheath Crossing was provided with a signal box (obscured by the tree on the left) until 15th August 1948. The long bridge span was due to the presence of the brickworks siding. (Lens of Sutton)

33. A later view from the footbridge seen in the previous photograph shows the 15.02 from Waterloo passing the crossing keeper's house on 24th September 1973. (J.Scrace)

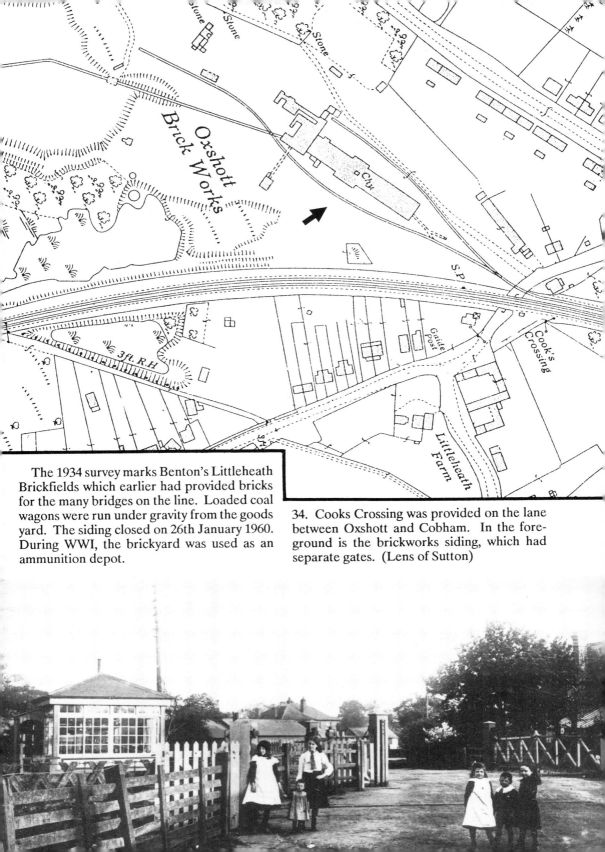

The 1934 survey marks Benton's Littleheath Brickfields which earlier had provided bricks for the many bridges on the line. Loaded coal wagons were run under gravity from the goods yard. The siding closed on 26th January 1960. During WWI, the brickyard was used as an ammunition depot.

34. Cooks Crossing was provided on the lane between Oxshott and Cobham. In the foreground is the brickworks siding, which had separate gates. (Lens of Sutton)

COOKS CROSSING

35. The crossing box became a block post on 22nd January 1961 and reverted to being a gate box when colour light signals were brought into use on 1st March 1970. A gate wheel was connected to the cranks in the foreground. Lifting barriers were fitted in September 1973, these being controlled from Surbiton Panel under CCTV from 28th April 1974. (J.Scrace)

36. Cooks Crossing up distant signal and Cobham up outer home are visible as two trains pass on the falling gradient (for down trains) caused by the Mole Valley. (Lens of Sutton)

COBHAM

37. The suffix "Stoke D'Abernon" referred to the nearby village and was officially in use from the opening of the line until September 1951. This southward view reveals that the ballast initially covered the sleepers, a practice soon to be condemned. (Lens of Sutton)

38. Looking north, at the height of the advertise-anywhere era, we note that homeward bound "daily breaders" had the comfort of a covered footbridge. In the distance, the points to the refuge siding can be seen. (Lens of Sutton)

39. Class M7 no. E107 arrives on 1st June 1925 with an up train composed of two 4-coach sets. The operating department had a great deal of experience with the limitations and advantages of set groups of coaches, long before electrification. (H.C.Casserely)

The map shows the optimum track layout, in 1934. A trailing siding was all that remained in 1990.

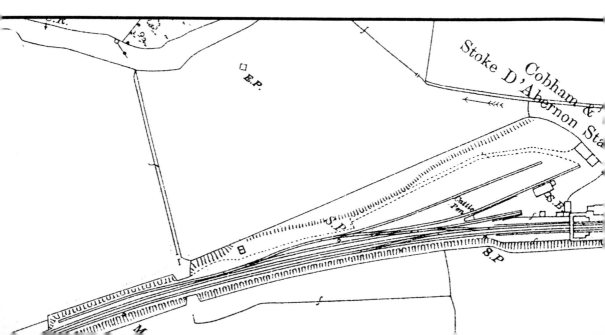

40. A 1941 photograph shows the short siding to the loading dock. SR features include the hexagonal lampshades and the upper quadrant signal, although this is mounted on an LSWR post. (D.Cullum coll.)

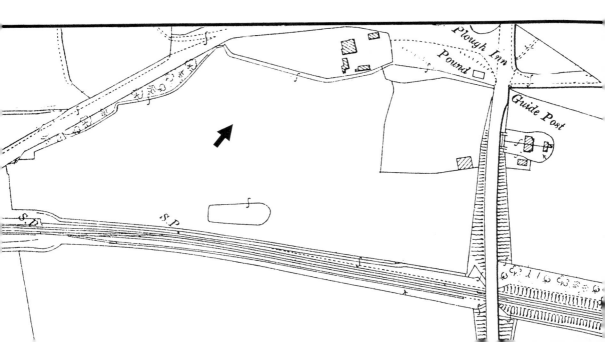

41. The signal box remained in use until 24th February 1966, the goods yard behind it having closed on 3rd May 1965. The goods shed was used by a plumbers' merchant, until it was demolished in 1989. (D.Cullum coll.)

42. After the flood waters of the River Mole had swept away a small bridge west of Cobham on 15th September 1968, trains from Waterloo terminated here and a bus link was provided to Effingham Junction. The station forecourt is occupied by a collection of vintage buses and coaches, on 21st September 1968. (J.N.Faulkner)

43. On the other side of the fence, 4SUB no. 4356 waits to return to Waterloo, having arrived at the down platform and used one of the trailing crossovers. The newspapers await collection beside a seasonal puddle. (J.N.Faulkner)

44. Station renovation was in progress on 19th May 1989 but the roof to the bridge had long gone. A waiting room seat stands in the open, retired and to be replaced by the chilling plastic coated, steel variety. (J.Scrace)

45. The crew are dazzled by the sun, as the 13.52 from Waterloo runs wrong-road on 13th December 1965, south of Cobham. Class 5 no. 73155 heads a ballast train required for the rectification of a slipped embankment.
(R.E.Ruffell)

LEATHERHEAD

46. A roadway was provided between the two railways, the LBSCR station being at the far end and that of the LSWR on the left. The latter's locomotives water column is also visible, but their small engine shed and turntable are not. (Lens of Sutton)

The complex railway history of the area can be simplified thus: the line north of Leatherhead became the joint property of the LBSCR and LSWR, a joint terminus being provided north of the town. When the LBSCR

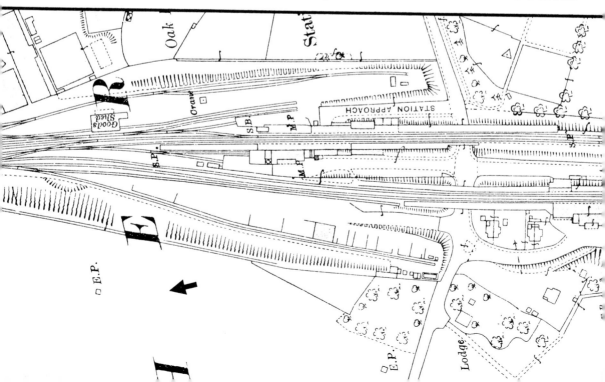

47. Looking north in 1925, we see the LSWR built goods shed and down platform on the left and the former LBSCR station and goods shed on the right. (Late E. Wallis)

continued south to Dorking, a new station was built further south and a separate terminal was erected alongside for the LSWR. This came into use on 4th March 1867 and is seen to the right of the page opposite, the two routes diverging on the left. This is the 1934 edition and shows that the ex-LSWR line had been truncated by then and a new junction made south of the ex-LBSCR platforms. The line to Dorking is on the right, while that to Bookham is lower right.

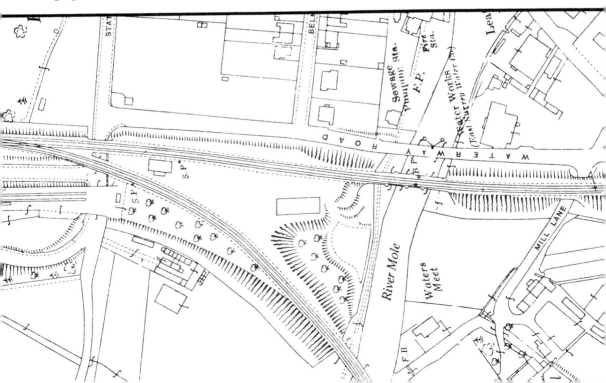

48. Viewed southwards, the ex-LBSCR goods yard is on the left, while that of the former LSWR is on the right in this April 1925 view. Conductor rails are mostly in place on both routes as electric services to Dorking North and to Effingham Junction commenced on the 12 July of that year. (Late E.Wallis)

49. The former LSWR station was closed on 10th July 1927 when a new junction, south of the LBSCR station, came into use. This view south shows that one electrified line was retained for berthing purposes.
(Lens of Sutton)

50. The west facade of the former LBSCR station is seen in about 1947, along with the lofty up starting signal and Mk.I telephone box. The splendid brickwork can still be enjoyed (Lens of Sutton)

51. When photographed in April 1970, the LSWR part of the station was completely disused. The locomotive shed had been situated in the distance but was demolished in about 1932. (R.E.Ruffell)

Other views and maps of this station can be seen in our *Epsom to Horsham* album.

52. The signal box was the sole survivor of the three that were in use until the 1927 track alterations. It still controlled the local colour light signals in 1990 but the vintage seat has been replaced. (Lens of Sutton)

53. Mechanical signalling was in use until 10th October 1971, the equipment being seen in 1960. The Effingham Junction line curves to the right of the substation, while electric stock is stabled on the former LSWR line. (D.Cullum)

54. The goods yard closed on 2nd August 1965 but the siding in the foreground was retained for the engineer's benefit. Two 4SUBs form the busy 07.49 Effingham Junction to Waterloo service on 12th June 1975. (J.Scrace)

55. To commemorate the end of a reign, the "508 Twilight" railtour was operated on 1st September 1984. Leatherhead signal box windows are visible as the train pauses on its tour from Waterloo via Hounslow, Nunhead, Slade Green, Brixton, East Putney, Hampton Court, Selhurst, Mitcham Junction, Wimbledon, Epsom, Horsham, Leatherhead, Effingham Junction, Guildford, Woking and Basingstoke. (A.Dasi-Sutton)

BOOKHAM

56. An early postcard depicts the station in its truly rural surroundings, on the southern fringe of Great Bookham Common. The villages of Little and Great Bookham are half a mile to the south. (Lens of Sutton)

57. A view towards Leatherhead includes the back of a throw-face shunt signal. The station was much used by ramblers and naturalists enjoying the delights the of nearby common. (Lens of Sutton)

```
┌─────────────────────────────────────────┐
│      London & South Western Ry.         │
│   This Ticket is issued subject to the Regulations │
│   & Conditions stated in the Company's Time │
│   Tables & Bills                         │
│   ─────────────────────────────────      │
│ 5859   EFFINGHAM JUNC. to   5859         │
│        BOOKHAM                           │
│   Effingham Junc.      Effingham Junc.   │
│     Bookham              Bookham         │
│   3rd CLASS   (S.2)    3rd CLASS         │
│   Fare 1½d            Fare 1½d           │
└─────────────────────────────────────────┘
```

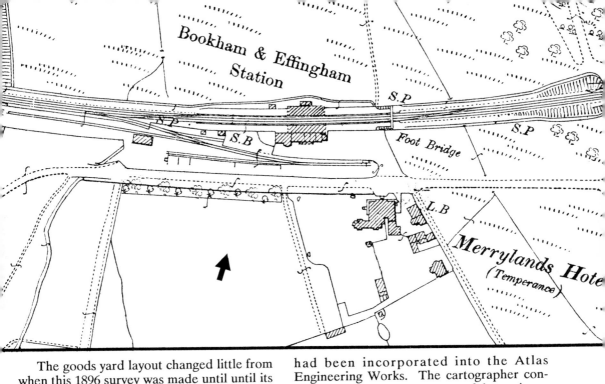

The goods yard layout changed little from when this 1896 survey was made until until its closure on 3rd May 1965. By 1934, the hotel had been incorporated into the Atlas Engineering Works. The cartographer continued to use the earlier name of the station.

58. A 1925 photograph shows new platform extensions and unused conductor rail. The up train is about to leave the down platform, probably having terminated there due to electrification works. The locomotive is class M7 0-4-4T no. 105. The July 1924 timetable showed two peak hour trains from London terminating here, apparently returning empty. (D.Cullum coll.)

59. The sign beyond the wagons in this 1958 photograph reads "Burn Neale's Coal". The two ton crane is adjacent to the goods shed, which did not have track into it. The crossover in the distance had earlier been located in the foreground. (British Rail)

60. Further platform improvements are evident in this 1968 photograph, as is the signal box which closed on 19th April 1969. The trees of the common almost encroached onto the platform by then. (J.Scrace)

61. The exterior is similar to most of the stations between Oxshott and London Road, having been opened on the same day, 2nd February 1885. It was devoid of a name when photographed in November 1989 (V.Mitchell)

The 1887 gradient profile marks the position of the spur to Surbiton, which was never built.

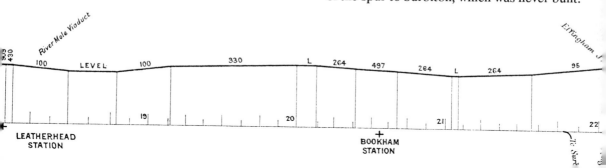

62. The 91yd long Bookham Tunnel is in the background as preparations were being made for driver only operation of trains in 1990. Two of the four down platform cameras hang from the canopy while there is a stand for three TV monitors, on the right. A further four were provided at the end of the platform, for use by drivers of 8-car trains. (V.Mitchell)

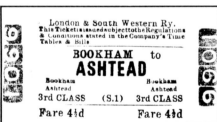

London & South Western Ry.
This Ticket is issued subject to the Regulations & Conditions stated in the Company's Time Tables & Bills

BOOKHAM to **ASHTEAD**

Bookham Ashtead   Bookham Ashtead

3rd CLASS   (S.1)   3rd CLASS

Fare 4½d   Fare 4½d

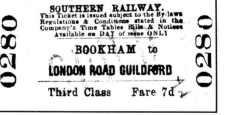

SOUTHERN RAILWAY.
This Ticket is issued subject to the By-laws Regulations & Conditions stated in the Company's Time Tables Bills & Notices Available on DAY of issue ONLY

BOOKHAM to **LONDON ROAD GUILDFORD**

Third Class   Fare 7d

64. A train from Cobham passes over the junction, just prior to the introduction of electric services. Power to the sub-station in the background was supplied from the SR's own generators at Durnsford Road, Wimbledon. (Lens of Sutton)

APPROACH TO
EFFINGHAM JUNCTION

63. As the line from Bookham curves towards Effingham Junction, the embankment for the incompleted triangular junction was still visible in 1953. (D.Cullum)

65. Approximately once a year a ramblers' excursion ran from Victoria to Cranleigh, hauled by steam motive power within the weight restrictions on the Guildford-Horsham line. On 25th June 1961, Q class 0-6-0 no.30549 comes off the Bookham line into Effingham Junction with one of these specials. (J.N.Faulkner)

66.   Hardy ramblers occupied this Victoria-Cranleigh excursion on 23rd February 1958. The class E1 4-4-0s nos. 31506 and 31067 weighed 53 tons each. (J.N.Faulkner)

67.   An RCTS railtour clatters over the junction on 18th June 1967, headed by no. 34023 *Blackmore Vale* (now on the Bluebell Railway) and piloted by class 5 4-6-0 no. 73029. The "Farewell to Steam" ran from Waterloo via Fareham, Swanage and Weymouth, returning to London via Eastleigh, Salisbury and Basingstoke. (J.Scrace)

EFFINGHAM JUNCTION

68. The station opened more than three years after the line, on 2nd July 1888. It served a thinly populated area, the village being nearly two miles to the south. The signal box is largely obscured by the central member of staff. (Lens of Sutton)

69. Unlike the other stations on the route, the minimum was spent on passenger accommodation, but the wooden buildings were easy targets for enamel sign fixers. The crossover had a companion beyond the far end of the platforms from 1897. (Lens of Sutton)

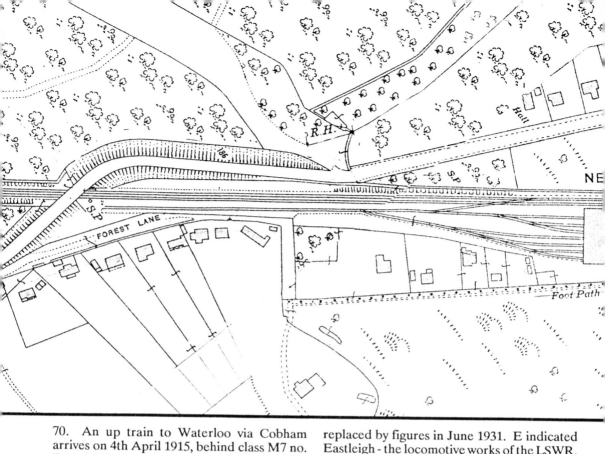

70. An up train to Waterloo via Cobham arrives on 4th April 1915, behind class M7 no. E24. Prefix letters were used by the SR until replaced by figures in June 1931. E indicated Eastleigh - the locomotive works of the LSWR. (H.C.Casserley)

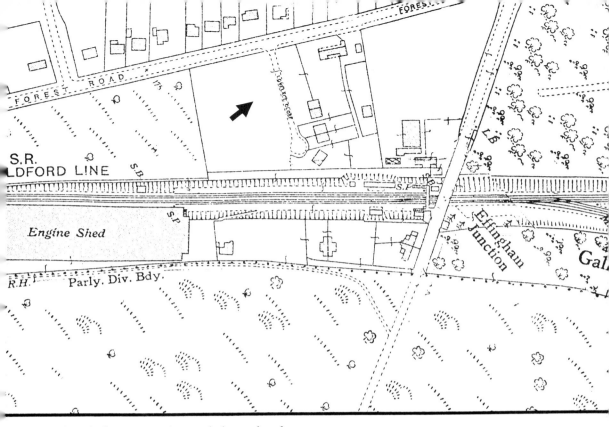

71. The platform extension and shunt signal are visible in this under exposed view of 3SUB no. 1236 in 1938. The headcode indicated Effingham Junction to Waterloo via Epsom. (D.H.Wakely/J.R.W.Kirkby coll.)

The 1934 survey has the junction of the Cobham and Bookham lines on the right and an incorrect description on the carriage shed, which was built in 1925 for the electric stock.

72. No. 73155 returns from the landslip site seen in picture no. 45, as 4SUB no. 4664 waits to cross its path as the 14.49 to Waterloo via Epsom. The 1885 signal box had served simply as a staff room since July 1925 and still did so in 1990. (R.E.Ruffell)

73. A 1955 view towards the junction shows the London end crossover, which was by then little used and was removed about three years later. (J.N.Faulkner)

74. The 08.20 Weymouth - Waterloo, already running via Netley and Havant, was further diverted over the New Guildford Line on 2nd April 1967 and is seen here passing Effingham Junction with class 33 diesel no. D6554 hauling two TC sets. The 1925 signal box is near the rear coaches. (J.N.Faulkner)

EFFINGHAM JUNCTION

OFF

75. The signal box faced the carriage shed and was in use from 11th July 1925 until 20th April 1969, when Guildford Panel took control of the area. The sign "OFF" was an instruction regarding 4SUB heaters, which were not thermostatically controlled. This photograph was taken in 1969. (J.Scrace)

76. The centre road runs only half the length of the shed and therefore takes only four cars. Terminating trains use the siding in the foreground and then return over the crossover to the up platform. Construction of the shed was not authorised until 26th March 1925 and so it was not ready for the commencement of electric services. (R.E.Ruffell)

77. Trains are cleaned internally in the shed daily but only the ends receive attention externally, the sides being washed mechanically at Wimbledon. The stencil carrier is being hosed down on 5th April 1974. (R.E.Ruffell)

78. The driver of a terminating train runs into the shunting neck on 13th April 1974, as 4VEP no. 7806 passes, forming the 10.52 Guildford to Waterloo. These units offered first class accommodation on the route at this time. Closure of the depot was scheduled for May 1990. (R.E.Ruffell)

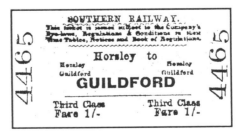

79. The booking hall and office are at road level and present a curious appearance when viewed from the up platform. A store room is provided at the lower level. (J.Scrace)

80. Introduced in 1979, the class 508 units had disc and rheostatic braking together with Tightlock couplers. Two four-car sets form the 11.43 departure on 10th July 1984, shortly before they were transferred to Merseyrail as three-car units. SR platform lighting still prevailed. (C.Wilson)

81. Direct access from road vehicles is unsatisfactory but steps are provided down to an extensive car park which occupies land on the down side, used earlier for five railway cottages - see map. The compact booking office is seen in November 1989. (V.Mitchell)

HORSLEY

82. The staff stand at ease in front of the 1903 footbridge. The station serves a large, scattered residential area, the old villages of East and West Horsley being more than one and two miles distant, respectively. (Lens of Sutton)

The siding arrangement shown on this 1934 map did not change during the life of the goods yard, which came to an end on 1st June 1964.

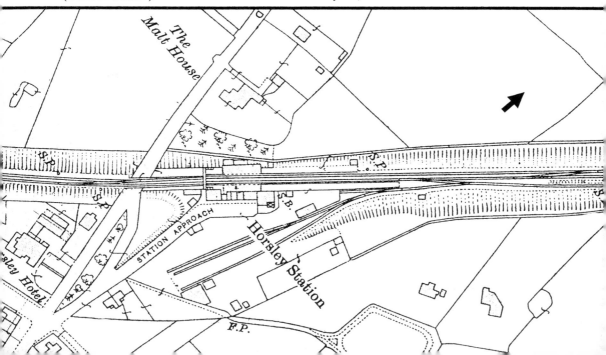

83. The line is level through the station but falls at 1 in 95 towards Effingham Junction, in the background. The siding in the distance was extended in 1897, to form a refuge siding. (Lens of Sutton)

84. This and the next two pictures were taken on 4th April 1925, at a time when the hourly Waterloo via Bookham service terminated here. This occurred from 1916 until 1925. One of these trains is standing in the refuge siding, while a Guildford service passes by. (H.C.Casserley)

85. Class M7 no. E674 waits by the water tank with a Waterloo via Epsom service, while a down freight occupies the other platform and wagons from the Great Central and North

Eastern Railways stand in the yard. Just visible
is the signal box, which closed on 4th July 1965.
(H.C.Casserley)

86. Horsley was the only intermediate station on the route to have a locomotive water supply. No. 674 is being replenished at the Guildford end of the down platform. (H.C.Casserley)

87. Two M7s pass on 1st June 1925. No. E27 runs over the road bridge, bound for Waterloo via Cobham, while no. E319 is held by the down starting signal. (H.C.Casserley)

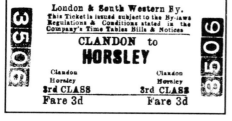

London & South Western Ry.
This Ticket is issued subject to the By-laws
Regulations & Conditions stated in the
Company's Time Tables Bills & Notices
CLANDON to
HORSLEY

Clandon	Clandon
Horsley	Horsley
3rd CLASS	3rd CLASS
Fare 3d	Fare 3d

88. The spacious station master's house, the large entrance canopy and the well ventilated gentlemen's toilet were features of the standard design, seen clearly at Horsley in July 1974. Subsequently, the roof light has been removed and bollards added, to protect the canopy from tall vehicles. (J.Scrace)

89. No. 50016 roars through the almost deserted station on 7th April 1979, heading the "Southern Invader", an ambitious railtour which started from Paddington and ran via Kensington Olympia, East Croydon, Redhill, Guildford, Wimbledon, East Putney, Lewisham, Oxted, Uckfield, Crystal Palace, Arundel, Eastleigh, Salisbury and Woking. (J.Scrace)

90. Since the growth of BR's unwanted linear woodland and the use of the trains devoid of sanding gear, special rail cleaning trains have become necessary. Unit no. 015 runs south on 27th November 1989 on its somewhat ineffective mission. (V.Mitchell)

91. Ex-LBSCR class C2X no. 32447 heads a down freight south of Horsley, on 26th July 1956. Note the coupling link substituting for a headcode disc. (R.C.J.Day)

CLANDON

92. An undated early view shows the approach road to be loose surfaced but the footway kerbs to be made from old running rails. Apart from the addition of a roof light, the building remained unaltered a century later.
(Lens of Sutton)

93. A pre-cast concrete footbridge is almost ready for use, the wooden one being of similar design to that still in use by the Wey Viaduct. The change over took place in about 1947.
(Patrick coll.)

94. The wooden-bodied first generation electric stock was largely withdrawn in the 1950s. The white bands on the canopy stanchions were applied during WWII, to make them more obvious during the blackout.
(Patrick coll.)

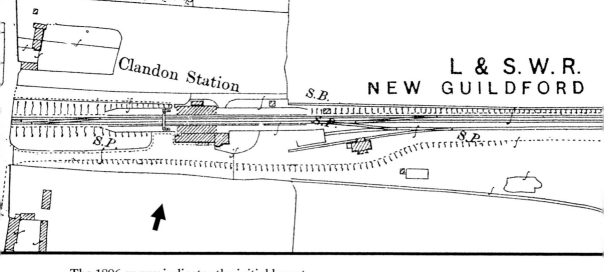

The 1896 survey indicates the initial layout. The headshunt was extended in 1897 and reduced in 1925.

95. Closure of the goods yard took place on 4th December 1963 and the signal box ceased to be used after 25th July 1965. The goods shed is seen (on the right) in April 1963, the building in the distance being the sub-station. (Patrick coll.)

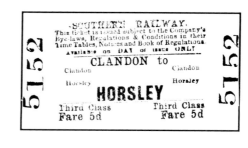

London & South Western Ry.

CLANDON · to

LEATHERHEAD

Clandon   Clandon
L'head   L'head

THIRD   **(S.1)**   THIRD
CLASS   See over   CLASS

Fare 8½d   Fare 8½d

96. The class 508 units were replaced by class 455s, built from 1982 to 1985 and introduced to the route in late 1984. The second coach, with the low roof line, was from one of the earlier 508 sets. No. 5726 forms the 12.56 from Guildford on 28th December 1985. (J.Scrace)

The 1934 map reveals an extra siding, terminating alongside the substation.

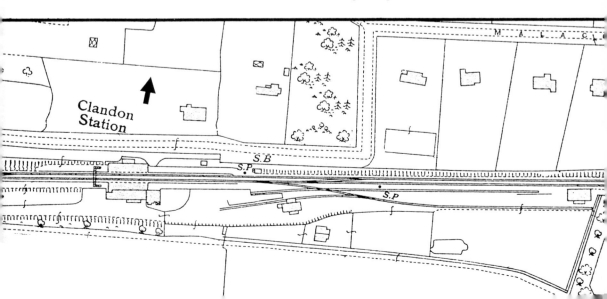

97. In 1987, heavy snow caused complete closure of the line on 14-15th January. A class 56 diesel from Westbury cleared the route with a snow plough on the 16th. It was the last notable snow of the decade. (C.Patrick)

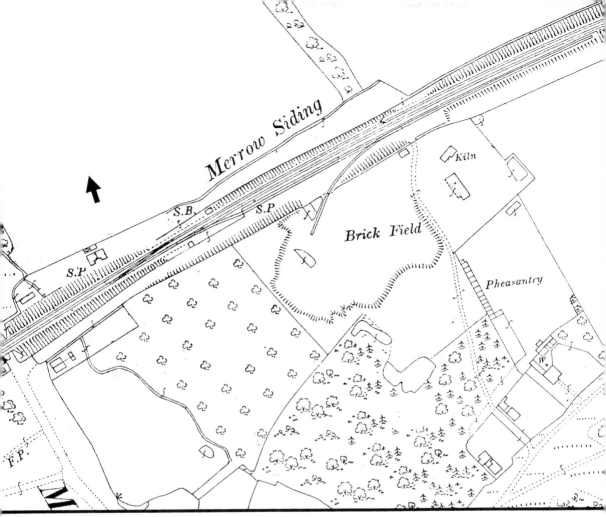

The 1914 survey marks the public siding, situated close to the Burpham - Merrow road (left). A private siding for Sutton & Co diverged from it, this later being used by Surrey County Council. The siding was shown on the first plans of the line and so it presumably carried bricks used in its construction. The signal box was closed on 13th March 1932, the siding being controlled by a ground frame until traffic ceased on 25th June 1961. Public goods services were withdrawn on 16th March 1960.

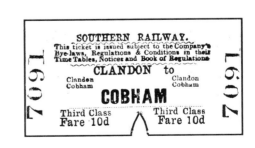

98. A 1989 view shows the station to be maintained in good order, although it is one of the least used on the route, there being a local population of only 1100. The crossover in the distance was retained for use by the engineers. (J.Scrace)

LONDON ROAD

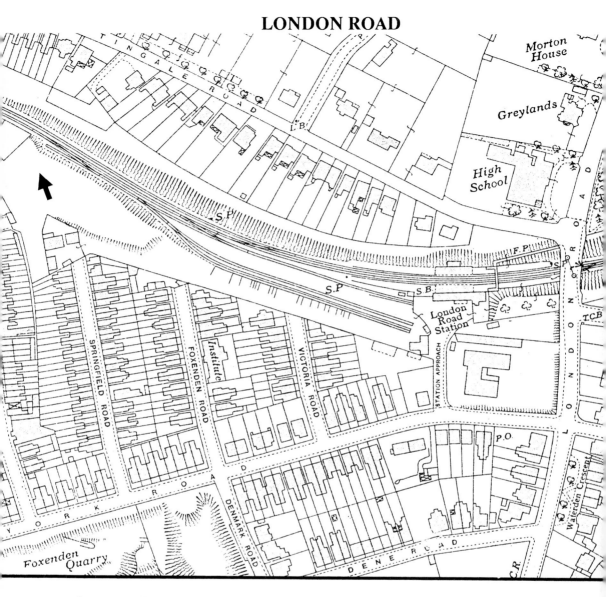

The 1934 edition marks three sidings but no goods shed, parcels being handled at the main station. The southernmost siding was not shown on the earlier maps. The signal box became a ground frame on 16th April 1966 and the goods yard closed on 6th January 1969, although a coal depot only since December 1965.

→

100. The 20 - chain curve has presented operational problems and is severe when compared with the 60 chain radius through Bookham station. The bridge carries London Road, once the main road between London and Portsmouth, and frames the inaugural train. (Patrick coll.)

99. The first electric train ran on Thursday 9th July 1925 and carried the Mayor and Mayoress of Guildford, SR officials and 300 guests. The special train left Waterloo at 10.8am and is seen returning after the opening ceremony, the goods yard being visible on the left. (Patrick coll.)

101. Situated in the northern suburbs of Guildford, the station was officially "London Road, Guildford" from 9th July 1923, as another London Road station was to be found on the SR, at Brighton. Introduced in 1957, one of the economical 2HAP units was an unusual visitor to the up platform on 5th March 1973. (R.E.Ruffell)

The 1920 survey at 6" to 1 mile marks London Road station on the right and the main station lower left. "Towing Path" indicates the position of the River Wey, which was navigable to Godalming - see *Surrey Waterways* (Middleton Press)

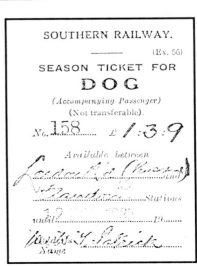

← 102. Class 455 units pass on 19th May 1989, a not uncommon occurrence as up and down trains were scheduled within four minutes of one another. A footpath, behind the fence on the right, gives direct access to the station from the north. (J.Scrace)

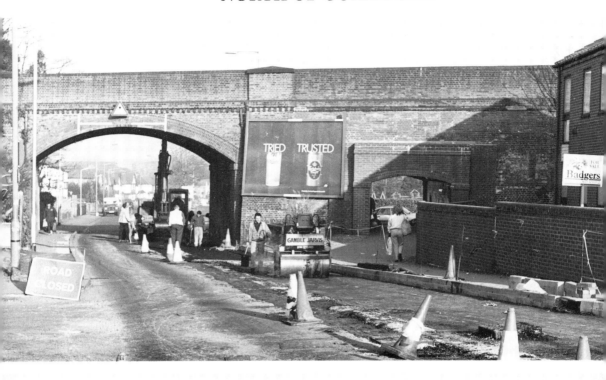

103. Stoke Road is the main road to Woking and was completely closed on 27th November 1989 to allow for resurfacing without decreasing the headroom. The pedestrian subway is a recent addition. The next bridge east (over Kings Road) has a clearance of only 10 ft 3 in. (V.Mitchell)

9758 9758

7 | 8 | 9 | 10 | 11 | 12
(No.1) SOUTHERN RAILWAY (S.12)
LONDON RD. GUILDFORD
The holder is prohibited from entering the Companies Trains. Not transferable
Admit ONE to PLATFORM 1ᴰ
Available ONE HOUR on DAY of ISSUE ONLY
1 | 2 | 3 | 4 | 5 | 6

104. The route crosses the Wey Valley on embankment and viaduct, the largest span of which is over the River Wey Navigation. The area is now fully developed with commercial premises (this book was printed in one of them) and the unusual cantilevered footbridge is now busier than the railway builders could have imagined. (V.Mitchell)

105. The final curve of the New Guildford Line is taken by the "Vectis Velocipede" on 21st June 1986. The train, organised by Hertfordshire Railtours, was composed of two class 105 units. The Woking line is in the centre background, while that to Reading and Aldershot curves away to the left. (A.Dasi-Sutton)

GUILDFORD

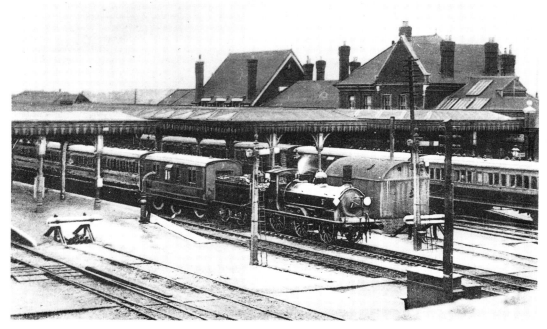

106. The cramped ill-conceived station, that had developed piecemeal since the branch from Woking opened in 1845, was replaced by the structure seen here. The rebuilding was undertaken in 1884, to accommodate the additional trains from the Guildford New Line. (Lens of Sutton)

107. Prior to WWII, many businesses owned coal wagons but seldom were two names shown on them. Mr Bonner was first listed as a coal merchant in 1907 but his only recorded relationship with the other firm was geographical - their respective premises were in close proximity. (HMRS coll.)

108. A semi-roundhouse locomotive depot was built at the same time as the new station. Its turntable and class A12 0-4-2 no. 654 were photographed on 20th September 1919. The shed had 13 radiating lines and closed on 9th July 1967. (K.Nunn/LCGB)

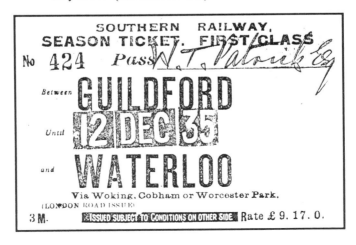

SOUTHERN RAILWAY.
SEASON TICKET. FIRST CLASS
No 424   Pass N. T. Patrick Esq
Between **GUILDFORD**
Until **12 DEC 35**
and **WATERLOO**
Via Woking, Cobham or Worcester Park.
(LONDON ROAD ISSUE)
3 M.   ISSUED SUBJECT TO CONDITIONS ON OTHER SIDE   Rate £ 9. 17. 0.

109. Class U1 no. A900 is running from Waterloo to Portsmouth on 20th August 1932. The train conceals the bay platform, added in 1925, for the New Guildford Line electric services. Until the electrification of the main line in 1937, it was the only platform line to have a conductor rail. (H.C.Casserley)

110. This undated photograph was taken between 1937 and 1947 and shows class D3 0-4-4T no. 2384 waiting in the South Box sidings, prior to returning to Horsham. The 1989 timetable allowed DMUs on the Redhill service to lay over in this siding. (J.Scrace coll.)

111. The massive goods shed remained standing until 1988, although the goods yard had closed in 1975. Chaplins were the authorised parcel agents for the SR and undertook local deliveries and collections. (E.Jackson)

113. To move dead engines in the roundhouse and perform other duties, a shed pilot was provided. In 1961, this was B4 class 0-4-0T no. 30089, one of a small class of engines designed for, and long used at, Southampton Docks. (D. Fereday Glenn)

112. On 18th September 1953, the driver of the 3.12pm from Waterloo failed to brake properly on entering platform 1 and demolished the station master's office and an adjacent one, causing six injuries and one fatality. The damage remained evident until the station was rebuilt in 1989. (British Rail)

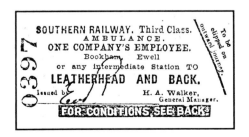

114. On the left is platform 1, the destination for most trains running via Cobham. At platform 3, 4-4-2T no. 30582 heads the Railway Enthusiasts Club's railtour on 19th March 1961. The platform canopies were cut back progressively, as the supports showed signs of failure. (Patrick coll.)

115. Class M7 no. 30132 accelerates south from platform 2 on 29th May 1961, bound for Horsham. Once familiar on the New Line, this class seldom worked to Horsham. No. 30132 had replaced a failed class E4 at short notice. Note that the horse box has both steam heating and vacuum brake connections, so that it can be included in passenger trains. (R.S.Greenwood)

116. Guildford has had trains to a variety of destinations. This is the 6.16pm to Dorking Town on 19th June 1961 headed by a goods engine, probably due to the absence of anything more suitable. It is a class 700 "Black Motor", no. 30690. (R.S.Greenwood)

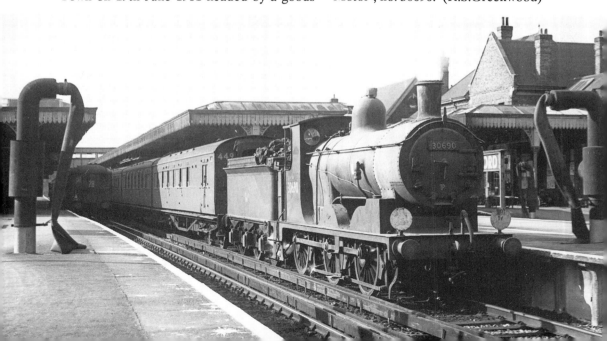

117. The basic hourly express service between London and Portsmouth was operated by the comfortable 4COR/4RES units from 1937 until 1970. Unit no. 3167 forms the 10.50 from Waterloo and is seen leaving platform 2 on 26th June 1969. (J.Scrace)

118. The 1884 building (centre background) became unusable and a temporary booking office was erected (right). Confusion in the restricted forecourt was compounded on 11th April 1987, when a replacement bus service was operating to North Camp, due to engineering works. (A.C.Mott)

119. Chaos was prolonged as rebuilding took most of 1988-89 to complete. Outside the peak hours, one or two platforms were closed and two trains frequently occupied the same platform, but without any destination indicators. This is the scene on 3rd August 1988, when only part of the canopy of platform 2 remained. (J.Scrace)

120. The new main entrance was in use when photographed on 31st October 1989, as was the rotating window cleaning platform above it. All the new platform canopies have similar devices. The £8m station was handling 22,000 passengers and 400 trains each weekday, in vastly improved surroundings. (V.Mitchell)

Other Middleton Press publications to feature this station are *Woking to Portsmouth, Branch Lines to Horsham, Reading to Guildford, Guildford to Redhill* **and** *Steaming Through Surrey.*

MP Middleton Press

Easebourne Lane, Midhurst. West Sussex. GU29 9AZ
(0730) 813169

BRANCH LINES

BRANCH LINES TO MIDURST
BRANCH LINES AROUND MIDHURST
BRANCH LINES TO HORSHAM
BRANCH LINES TO EAST GRINSTEAD
BRANCH LINES TO ALTON
BRANCH LINE TO HAYLING
BRANCH LINE TO SOUTHWOLD
BRANCH LINE TO TENTERDEN
BRANCH LINES TO NEWPORT
BRANCH LINES TO TUNBRIDGE WELLS
BRANCH LINE TO SWANAGE
BRANCH LINES TO LONGMOOR
BRANCH LINE TO LYME REGIS
BRANCH LINE TO FAIRFORD
BRANCH LINE TO ALLHALLOWS
BRANCH LINES AROUND ASCOT
BRANCH LINES AROUND WEYMOUTH
BRANCH LINE TO HAWKHURST
BRANCH LINES AROUND EFFINGHAM JNC

SOUTH COAST RAILWAYS

CHICHESTER TO PORTSMOUTH
BRIGHTON TO EASTBOURNE
RYDE TO VENTNOR
EASTBOURNE TO HASTINGS
PORTSMOUTH TO SOUTHAMPTON
SOUTHAMPTON TO BOURNEMOUTH
ASHFORD TO DOVER
BOURNEMOUTH TO WEYMOUTH

SOUTHERN MAIN LINES

HAYWARDS HEATH TO SEAFORD
EPSOM TO HORSHAM
CRAWLEY TO LITTLEHAMPTON
THREE BRIDGES TO BRIGHTON
WATERLOO TO WOKING
VICTORIA TO EAST CROYDON
TONBRIDGE TO HASTINGS
EAST CROYDON TO THREE BRIDGES
WOKING TO SOUTHAMPTON
WATERLOO TO WINDSOR
LONDON BRIDGE TO EAST CROYDON

COUNTRY RAILWAY ROUTES

BOURNEMOUTH TO EVERCREECH JNC
READING TO GUILDFORD
WOKING TO ALTON
BATH TO EVERCREECH JUNCTION
GUILDFORD TO REDHILL
EAST KENT LIGHT RAILWAY
FAREHAM TO SALISBURY
BURNHAM TO EVERCREECH JUNCTION
REDHILL TO ASHFORD

LONDON SUBURBAN RAILWAYS

CHARING CROSS TO DARTFORD

STEAMING THROUGH

STEAMING THROUGH KENT
STEAMING THROUGH EAST HANTS
STEAMING THROUGH SURREY
STEAMING THROUGH WEST SUSSEX
STEAMING THROUGH THE ISLE OF WIGHT
STEAMING THROUGH WEST HANTS

OTHER RAILWAY BOOKS

WAR ON THE LINE
GARRAWAY FATHER & SON
LONDON CHATHAM & DOVER RAILWAY
INDUSTRIAL RAILWAYS OF THE S. EAST
WEST SUSSEX RAILWAYS IN THE 1980S

OTHER BOOKS

MIDHURST TOWN THEN & NOW
EAST GRINSTEAD THEN & NOW

WALKS IN THE WESTERN HIGH WEALD

MILITARY DEFENCE OF WEST SUSSEX
SUSSEX POLICE FORCES

SURREY WATERWAYS
KENT AND EAST SUSSEX WATERWAYS